PHONICS

ACTIVITIES

Sandra Fisher
Carole Palmer
Susan Bloom
Joyce Stirniman

CONSULTANT
Elizabeth C. Stull, Ph.D.

ILLUSTRATOR
Anne Kennedy

PUBLICATIONS INTERNATIONAL, LTD.

Elizabeth C. Stull holds a doctorate in early and middle childhood education specializing in curriculum and supervision. She has taught language, literacy, and children's literature at Ohio State University and has written numerous activity books for teachers, including *Alligators to Zebras: Whole Language Activities for the Primary Grades, Kindergarten Teachers Survival Guide,* and *Multicultural Learning Activities: K–6.*

Sandra Fisher (M.A.) works at Kutztown University (PA) as an assistant professor of elementary education and coordinator of the Early Learning Center. She has more than 25 years of classroom experience and has served as vice president of the National Organization of Campus Development Laboratory Schools and as editor of the *NOCDLS Bulletin.*

Carole Palmer (M.A.) is a reading specialist. Previously a first-grade teacher, she writes educational material for children, including curricula for reading programs, spelling series, and phonics projects.

Susan Bloom (M.A.) is a writer and editor for Creative Services Associates, Inc., a publisher of educational materials.

Joyce Stirniman is a writer and editor for Creative Services Associates, Inc. She has also served as field manager for the National Assessment of Education Progress—The Nation's Report Card.

ISBN: 0-4127-0066-3

CONTENTS

FIRST WORDS

▼▼▼

Reading is a skill, and perhaps the most important skill a child can learn. Although a number of methods are used for teaching reading, the phonics method is one of the most effective. With the phonics method, the child learns that sounds correspond to alphabet letter symbols. Using these letter sounds, words can be "decoded" and read.

Children can learn letters and their corresponding letter sounds with *101 Phonics Activities*. Children are active learners. These phonics activities are designed so the child will be learning by "doing," by using senses, and by asking questions. The book is intended for preschoolers, ages three to six, but children slightly younger and older can benefit from the book's activities as well.

To stimulate the child's interest in reading, you must provide a print-rich environment filled with books, magazines, and newspapers. It is important that the child sees you reading and that you read to the child for pleasure. For practical purposes and for use with this book, it is a good idea to make letter cards: Print the upper- and lowercase forms of one letter on each of 26 index cards.

Oral communication is also important for language development. Listen to what the child is saying. Talk with him or her as much as possible. With you as a role model, the child will develop good listening and speaking patterns and an interest in learning and reading.

This book is divided into seven chapters. Each chapter has activities designated as "easy" (one handprint), "medium" (two handprints), or "challenging" (three handprints). These activity levels are built on the hierarchy of language and reading development.

easy	*medium*	*challenging*

The "easy" level lays the foundation for basic skills; children manipulate objects and call attention to beginning sounds of words. On the "medium" level, the child begins to associate letter symbols and letter sounds through listening skills, letter recognition, and tactile experiences. The activities on the "challenging" level require applying letter symbols to letter sounds and using fine motor skills. Children learn at different rates. You may find that the child needs an easier or more challenging activity from one chapter to another.

As you preview these activities, remember that they need not be done in a sequential manner. You should alternate activities, skipping from chapter to chapter, so that the child will have experiences that range from art to cooking to manipulating objects. Read all the materials, the directions, and words of caution for every activity. All of the activities require *direct* adult supervision because of the materials used (such as scissors) or the nature of the activity (for example, cooking). Also be sure to clean yourselves and your work area before and after doing these projects.

As you and the child select an activity, discuss what you are going to do. Talk with the child while he or she is working on a particular project. Be patient, and praise the child as he or she is doing an activity. You may also find it helpful to repeat an activity from time to time. The projects are designed so that they can be enjoyed again and again.

Chapter 1: Sounds Like Fun. With these activities, children reinforce their command of beginning-letter sounds and listening skills.

Chapter 2: A B See. Here, the child learns to recognize printed letters.

Chapter 3: Eye to Hand. With these activities, the child learns letter recognition and also develops the small-muscle coordination necessary for writing.

Chapter 4: Word Sense. With these activities, many of which are challenging, children apply their knowledge of letter sounds and recognition to beginning reading.

Chapter 5: Alphabet Cooking. With the activities in this chapter, children will learn letter sounds while doing two of their favorite things—cooking and eating.

Chapter 6: Alphabet Arts & Crafts. Here, the child uses art materials to explore sounds and letters.

Chapter 7: Alphabet Adventures. The exciting phonics activities in this chapter will help the child learn letter sounds and word recognition while being active.

Most of all, have fun with the activities. The more enjoyable the phonics activities are for children, the more they'll want to do them—and the faster they'll learn to read.

SOUNDS LIKE FUN

A GORGEOUS GIFT

▼▼

A surprise awaits you when you open this gorgeous gift.

What You'll Need: Box that can be closed, ribbon, gift item that begins with the letter *G*

People enjoy giving gifts almost as much as they enjoy receiving them. This activity lets the child select a gift to give to you, making the exercise an educational experience as well.

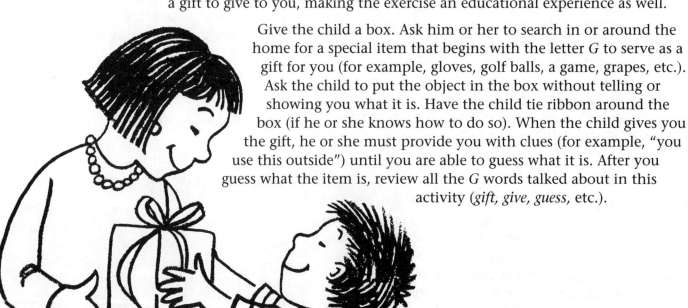

Give the child a box. Ask him or her to search in or around the home for a special item that begins with the letter *G* to serve as a gift for you (for example, gloves, golf balls, a game, grapes, etc.). Ask the child to put the object in the box without telling or showing you what it is. Have the child tie ribbon around the box (if he or she knows how to do so). When the child gives you the gift, he or she must provide you with clues (for example, "you use this outside") until you are able to guess what it is. After you guess what the item is, review all the *G* words talked about in this activity (*gift, give, guess,* etc.).

 # TO RHYME OR NOT TO RHYME

▼▼

Here's a rhyming game that helps a child develop important language skills.

Being able to hear different sounds in a series of words is an important skill that can be developed in young children.

First explain what a rhyme is. Use a series of two words that sound alike, such as *bat* and *cat* or *dog* and *log*. Once that concept is clear, say three words—two that rhyme and one that does not, such as *bat, cat, mop*. Ask the child to identify the word that doesn't rhyme. (Change the order of words occasionally so that the nonrhyming word isn't always the last word in the group.)

Next, try saying four words—three words that rhyme and one word that doesn't, in any order (for example, *tree, bird, free, key*)—and ask the child if he or she can identify the word that doesn't rhyme. If the child is having difficulty picking the nonrhyming word, have him or her repeat all four words. If the child has trouble recalling all of the words, repeat the list to him or her.

PHONICS FUN FACT

The Greeks were the first people to form and to use a true alphabet. The English word *alphabet* is composed of the first two letters of the Greek alphabet, *alpha* and *beta*.

RUN, WALK, JUMP, AND HOP

Hop for happiness and jump for joy in this beginning-sound activity.

Play an active game that focuses on the beginning sounds *H, R, W,* and *J.*

Say the word *hand,* and ask the child to demonstrate hopping. Point out that the words *hand* and *hop* begin with the same sound. Tell the child that you will say words that begin like *hop* and also some that begin like *run, walk,* and *jump.* He or she should perform the activity (hop, run, walk, or jump) that has the same beginning sound as the word you say. Words to use might include *rope, wet, jar, head, win, jet, red,* and *hat.*

RECORDING STAR

Every child will feel like a star hearing his or her own voice on a tape recorder.

What You'll Need: Tape recorder

Tape-recording helps reinforce recognition of beginning sounds by using the child's own voice.

Say a simple sentence that includes two words that begin with the same sound. For example, "Mom put the *jelly* in the *jar.*" Turn the tape recorder on, and have the child repeat the sentence, then have him or her say the two words that begin alike. Play the recording for the child. Then continue with new sentences.

SNAP LETTERS

Instead of using those clothespins on a clothesline, try snapping them on pictures.

What You'll Need: Lightweight cardboard, compass, felt-tip pen, blunt scissors, old magazine, glue or clear tape, eight snap clothespins

This activity reinforces eight different beginning sounds.

Take a piece of lightweight cardboard, and using a compass, draw and cut out a circle approximately 8″ wide. Use the pen to divide the circle into eight equal sections, as if it were a pie. Next, cut out eight pictures of familiar objects from a magazine (for example, ball, pen, fish, dog, carrot, hat, shoe, and apple). Make sure that each picture is small enough to fit into one section of the circle and that no two objects begin with the same letter. Glue or tape the pictures in place.

On the opening end of each snap clothespin, write a letter that matches the first letter of the object in each picture (in our example, the letters *B, P, F, D, C, H, S,* and *A*). Ask the child to take each lettered clothespin and snap it onto the section of the circle that has an object whose name begins with the same letter. Continue until all the letter matches are made.

If the child has difficulty with certain letters, focus on those letters the next time you do this activity. (Hint: You can use the back of the circle and the other side of the clothespins to repeat this activity with a new set of letters.)

CIRCLE KITES

▼▼

Tell kids to go fly a kite—and learn about the letter K.

What You'll Need: Kraft paper, blunt scissors, compass, crayons, tissue paper or crepe paper, yardstick, glue or clear tape, hole puncher, string

This activity helps children become familiar with *K*, a rarely used beginning letter.

Cut a circle with a diameter of about 12″ to 18″ from the kraft paper. Ask the child to write *K* and *k* on the paper circle, then identify three things that begin with the *K* sound (for example, a kangaroo, key, and kettle).

Make 8 or 10 streamers, approximately 1″×18″, out of colorful tissue paper or crepe paper. Help the child glue or tape the ends of the streamers around the bottom edge of the paper circle. Punch two small holes in the center of the circle, then put a string approximately 24″ long through the holes, tying it so that the string is on the opposite side of the kite from the streamers. As the child runs outside, pulling the kite with the string, the streamers will float behind.

PHONICS FUN FACT
English is a growing language. At the turn of the 20th century, words were added at the rate of 1,000 per year. Now, the increase is closer to 15,000 to 20,000 words per year.

LETTER LONDON BRIDGE

London Bridge is falling down—unless kids can identify beginning sounds.

What You'll Need: Index cards, old magazines, blunt scissors, glue or clear tape

Here's a new slant on an old singing game that will help children practice letter sounds.

Make picture cards by cutting out pictures of simple objects from magazines and gluing or taping them onto index cards. To play the game, sing "London Bridge Is Falling Down" with a small group of children. The players walk one by one through the bridge formed by two other players. When the song ends, the player inside the bridge is "caught." In order to be "released," he or she looks at a picture card, identifies it, and then gives a word with the same first-letter sound as the object in the picture.

THUMBS-UP

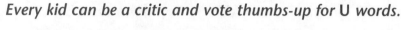

*Every kid can be a critic and vote thumbs-up for **U** words.*

Use hand motions to emphasize words that begin with the letter *U*.

Have the child demonstrate the gestures for thumbs-up and thumbs-down. Explain that when you say a word, he or she should show thumbs-up if the word begins with the letter *U* or point thumbs-down if it does not. Words to use might include *apple, desk, ugly, under, off,* and *umbrella*.

LETTER FOR THE DAY

Check your calendar to find out what special letter day it is.

What You'll Need: Calendar

Not sure what to do, say, wear, or eat on a particular day? Let this activity help you.

You will need a calendar. Ask the child to randomly pick a letter of the alphabet for each square that represents a day of the month. Each night, ask the child to think of things that could be done the next day beginning with that particular letter. Using the letter *B* for an example, you could *bounce* a *ball, bake,* or *blow bubbles.* You could also eat *butter, bread,* or a *banana,* or wear something *blue, brown,* or *black.* Encourage the child to say all the *B* words he or she can think of.

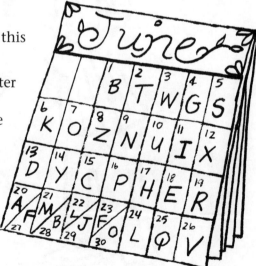

PICTURE DICTIONARY

▼▼▼

Make a special book for a special person.

What You'll Need: Old magazines, 26 sheets of 8½″×11″ construction paper of various colors, marker, blunt scissors, glue or clear tape, hole puncher, yarn

Have the child design a Picture Dictionary filled with pictures of things that are of interest to him or her. For example, if the child likes sports, use several old sports magazines for this project.

Write both the capital and lowercase forms of one letter of the alphabet in the upper right corner of each of the 26 sheets of construction paper. Give the child an old magazine and blunt scissors, and ask him or her to look for and cut out pictures of things that begin with each letter of the alphabet. Help the child glue or tape a picture on the correct letter page. When all or most of the pages have pictures on them, help the child make a front and back cover. Punch holes on the left side of each page, then bind the pages with yarn.

PHONICS FUN FACT
The most widely used letters in written English are
e, t, a, o, i, n, s, r, h, and *l.*

LISTEN CAREFULLY

▼▼

One word in a group is not like the others. Which is it?

Select a letter of the alphabet, and think of some words that begin with the sound of that same letter. Tell the child that you will be saying three words—two words that begin with the same sound and one word that is different. Say the three words (for example, *cat, ball, bird*). Have the child listen carefully and then tell you which word begins with the different letter sound.

Variation: To make this activity more challenging, say four or five words with the same beginning letter sound and one that is different. You can also reverse roles and have the child think of words that begin similarly and differently.

SMELLS GOOD!

▼▼

Let kids' noses lead them through this initial-letter activity.

What You'll Need: Variety of foods and other items with identifiable smells (as described below), scarf or blindfold

Children put their noses to work in this beginning-sound activity.

Collect several foods and other items with interesting smells, such as a slice of apple sprinkled with cinnamon, a lemon, an orange slice, a bar of soap, a bottle of perfume, toothpaste, a sprig of mint, a tea bag, an onion slice, and a banana.

Blindfold the child, and let him or her smell an item and try to identify it. Then the child must say another word that begins with the same sound. For an added challenge, ask the child to say the letter that begins the name of the item.

LOOK AT ME

Watch what happens when you talk into a mirror.

What You'll Need: Mirror

Mirrors are fascinating to children. This activity allows them to see what lip and mouth movements occur when different words are spoken.

Tell the child various words, and have him or her repeat them while looking in a mirror (for example, *dog* for a *D* sound, *button* for a *B* sound, *milk* for an *M* sound, *tooth* for a *T* sound, *pat* for a *P* sound, and so on). As each word is said, ask the child if his or her lips touched (as when saying words that begin with *B*, *M*, and *P*). And where was "Mr. Tongue?" Was he touching the front teeth, on the roof of the mouth, or hiding inside?

Ask the child to think of other words that begin with a particular letter and say them to the mirror, seeing if his or her mouth formations are the same for each letter sound.

ALPHABET WORD CHALLENGE

How many words can you think of that begin with a certain letter?

What You'll Need: Alphabet cards

After the child learns the alphabet and its letter sounds, this activity will provide a good review of letters and their sounds.

Show the child a letter of the alphabet. The challenge is for the child to name as many things as he or she can beginning with that letter. If a letter has different sounds (for example, the letter *C*, which can be hard or soft), encourage the child to use words with all the possible sounds of that particular letter.

A B SEE

LETTER SEARCH

Have fun looking at pictures to find special hidden letters.

What You'll Need: Pictures from an old magazine or travel brochure, pen or marker

This activity allows a child to look for hidden letters and then make a word out of them.

Take a picture from a magazine or travel brochure. Using a pen or marker, hide some letters in the photograph by blending all or parts of them into the lines, curves, and shapes of objects in the picture. Ideally, the letters must be written so that they are visible, yet thin enough so that the child's search will be somewhat challenging.

One way to start is to use the letters in the child's name. Try capital letters first and then lowercase letters. Give the child the picture, and have him or her search for the letters in his or her name. When the letters are found, ask the child to say each one and show where it is.

ALPHABET AVENUE

▼▼▼

Kids can walk the walk and talk the talk on this educational street.

What You'll Need: Butcher paper, marker

On a large sheet of butcher paper, print two or three large letters with a marker. Make each letter approximately two feet high. You might start with the vowels *A, E, I, O,* and *U* or with the consonants *B, D, P, S,* and *T.* Put the sheet on the floor, and ask the child to walk on or around each letter while saying its name. After the child has mastered these letters, make a new sheet with new letters.

LETTER SCULPTURE

▼▼▼

Mold youngsters' minds with three-dimensional letters.

What You'll Need: Shoe box, sand, plaster of paris, water

Making three-dimensional letters enables a child to experience the alphabet in a new way.

Put some moist sand in a shoe box. Help the child write letters in the sand. Let the child choose the letters to write, such as the initials of his or her first and last name. Make the letter shapes in the sand deep and wide. Mix the plaster of paris according to the directions on the package, and pour it into the letter shapes. Let the letters dry. Take the letters out of the box, and display your three-dimensional letters.

MEMORIES

▼▼

Make a keepsake album of a special field trip.

What You'll Need: Camera, glue or clear tape, paper, pen, hole puncher, string

A field trip can be a rewarding experience for a child. In this activity, a lesson on language is incorporated into the experience.

Select a special place to visit with the child (for example, a zoo, a farm, or a circus). While on this trip, have the child take photographs. (Your assistance may be needed with the camera.) After the film has been developed, the child can glue or tape the photos on paper. Allow space for captions.

Have the child dictate a sentence to describe what happened in each photo. Write this description below each photo so the child sees the process of sounding out letters and putting them in written (printed) form. Punch holes in each page, and using string, tie the pages together to form a book. Save a special photo for the cover, then decide on a title for the book and write it on the cover. The child now has a special book about a special trip.

STEPPING STONES

▼▼

Take these "steps" to learn letters and sounds.

What You'll Need: 26 sheets of paper, markers

Let the child explore the many possibilities of this activity.

Write a capital *A* on one side of a sheet of paper and a lowercase *a* on the other side. Do the same for each letter of the alphabet. Spread the sheets of paper on the floor like stones, and see how the child uses these materials. He or she can arrange them in alphabetical order or make a long path and say each letter as it is stepped on.

LETTERS IN THE MAIL

Open your own post office to reinforce letter recognition.

What You'll Need: Alphabet cards, six blank envelopes, six shoe boxes, crayon or marker, drawing paper

Children can learn letters and increase their dexterity by creating their own "mail."

Hold up an alphabet card. Have the child use a crayon or marker to write the letter on an envelope and on the side of one of the shoe boxes. Ask the child to draw a picture of an object whose name begins with the letter on the envelope. Show the child how to fold the drawing, put it into the envelope, and seal the envelope (or put the flap inside the envelope).

Follow the same procedure until you have six different drawings in six envelopes, each one representing a different letter, and six shoe boxes, each one with a letter matching an envelope on its side. Shuffle the six "letters," and have the child "mail" each one in the appropriate shoe box. The next day, the child can receive his or her mail, further reinforcing letter recognition skills.

PHONICS FUN FACT

Fifteen capital letters are called stick letters and are made with horizontal, vertical, or diagonal lines: *A, E, F, H, I, K, L, M, N, T, V, W, X, Y,* and *Z.* Circle letters include *O, Q,* and *C.*

NATURAL LETTERS

▼▼▼▼▼▼▼▼▼▼▼▼▼▼▼▼▼▼▼▼▼▼▼▼▼▼▼▼▼▼▼▼▼▼▼▼

Your environment is a source for many letter shapes. How many can you find?

Many letters of the alphabet can be seen if one looks closely at different objects.

Ask the child questions such as: *Inside the house, is the letter* H *visible if you look at the legs of a chair? Do you see a* Y *when looking at the branches of a plant? Outdoors, can you see an* L *by looking at the side of the steps? Can you see an* A *in the frame of your swing set?* See how many letters you can find in your environment.

PICK A NUMBER

▼▼▼▼▼▼▼▼▼▼▼▼▼▼▼▼▼▼▼▼▼▼▼▼▼▼▼▼▼▼▼▼▼▼▼▼

All numbers are lucky when kids use them to learn letters.

What You'll Need: Paper, ten cards with numbers 1 through 10, pen or pencil

This activity helps children recognize both letters and numbers.

On a sheet of paper, write the numbers 1 through 10 in a column, and write a letter by each number. Shuffle the number cards, and place them in a stack. Instruct the child to take the top card, match it to a number on the sheet, and name the corresponding letter.

If the child identifies the letter correctly, he or she keeps the number card. If the child is incorrect, the card is placed at the bottom of the stack. When all the letters have been identified correctly, make a list with different letters.

WHERE WAS IT?

▼▼

Test your memory, and find the matching letter.

What You'll Need: 16 paper cards (2″×2″ each), a pen or marker

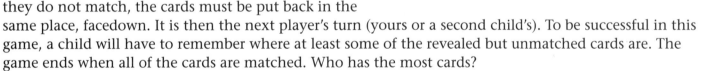

Use this activity to enhance a child's visual memory.

Make a set of two alphabet cards for each of any eight letters. Depending on the child's developmental level, the matching cards may both be capital letters (*A* and *A*) or lowercase letters (*a* and *a*), or else a combination of the two (*A* and *a*).

Shuffle the 16 cards (eight pairs of letters), and arrange them facedown in a square (four rows of four). Ask the child to turn over any two cards. If they match, he or she can keep that set and take another turn. If they do not match, the cards must be put back in the same place, facedown. It is then the next player's turn (yours or a second child's). To be successful in this game, a child will have to remember where at least some of the revealed but unmatched cards are. The game ends when all of the cards are matched. Who has the most cards?

DON'T LOOK NOW

Pin the tail on the...alphabet?

What You'll Need: Poster board or butcher paper, marker, removable tape, scarf to be used as a blindfold

Here's a twist on an old party favorite, pin the tail on the donkey. Use a marker to print the letters of the alphabet in random order on the poster board or butcher paper. Tape this letter chart to the back of a door.

Cover the child's eyes with the scarf, and turn him or her around two or three times. Tell the child to locate and put a finger on the chart. Take off the blindfold, and have the child identify the letter he or she is touching. Repeat until several different letters have been identified.

PHONICS FUN FACT

The English alphabet is one of about 50 alphabets in the modern world. Although these alphabets may differ in the number and design of their letters, they all are based on the idea of using symbols to represent the sounds of language.

MENU SPECIALS

Waiting for your food to be served? This menu game helps time pass quickly.

What You'll Need: Menu

What can you do in a restaurant to involve a child until dinner is served? Keep your menu, and play this game.

Ask the waiter or waitress if you may keep the menu until dinner is served. Give the child the menu, and have him or her locate a menu item beginning with a certain letter. You can be specific and state that it must be a capital or lowercase letter. When the child finds a word beginning with that letter, have him or her point to it and say the letter. Ask the child to look at all the letters in the word and, by sounding out the letters, try to determine what the menu item is.

WHERE IS IT?

How many objects can you find in your home starting with a particular letter of the alphabet?

What You'll Need: Alphabet cards

An important step in learning to read is to be able to match a letter to its letter sound and to objects whose names have such sounds.

Hand the child an alphabet card (for example, the letter *D*). Ask him or her to look around the home for an object beginning with that letter (for example, a doll). Have the child say the letter and name the object to verify the match.

ALPHABET PHOTO ALBUM

Neighborhood adventurers and photography enthusiasts will find this activity eye-opening.

What You'll Need: Camera, scrapbook or photo album

This is an exciting outdoor activity that helps children learn the alphabet—as well as operate a camera.

Get a camera (a disposable one will do), and go on a walk through the neighborhood or a nearby town or city with the child. Ask him or her to look for each letter of the alphabet on as many different street signs and store signs as possible. Take one picture of each letter found. You might want to show the child how to use the camera so he or she can help shoot the photos.

Don't try to get the whole alphabet in one outing. Develop the pictures, and help the child put them in a scrapbook or album in alphabetical order. Enjoy one or two more outings in which you look for the specific letters you're missing to complete the set.

TELEPHONE DIRECTORY

▼▼▼

Find names beginning with different letters using an old phone directory.

What You'll Need: Old telephone directory, blunt scissors, envelope

Another source where many letters are found is a telephone directory.

Show the child an old telephone directory, and look through it together. Explain what is in a telephone directory. Have the child recognize that names always begin with a capital letter, that a telephone directory lists last names first, and that the book is arranged in alphabetical order. A good introduction to the directory is to look for and cut out the child's last name or a friend's name. Using blunt scissors, the child can also cut out names beginning with each letter of the alphabet. (You can use bold-faced names for easier cutting and viewing—or cut out groups of five or more consecutive names.) After the names are cut out and every letter has been found, place these cuttings in an envelope, saving them for the activity titled Telephone Directory II.

TELEPHONE DIRECTORY II

▼▼▼

Forgot a telephone number? This directory can help.

What You'll Need: Names cut out for Telephone Directory activity, sheet of paper, glue or clear tape

Have the child use the names in the envelope that were cut out for Telephone Directory. The object now is for the child to organize these names in alphabetical order. (It may be easier for the child to spread all the names on the floor or table.)

When the names are arranged in alphabetical order, have the child begin with the name that comes first in alphabetical order and glue or tape it onto the paper. Proceed through the alphabet. The names can be arranged as in a real telephone directory—in columns, proceeding from top to bottom and left to right.

BOWLING FOR SCHOLARS

Children who know their letters can bowl a perfect game.

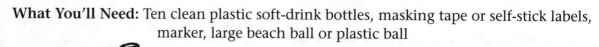

What You'll Need: Ten clean plastic soft-drink bottles, masking tape or self-stick labels, marker, large beach ball or plastic ball

This activity combines bowling and letter identification.

Put a strip of masking tape or a label on each bottle, and print a different letter on each one. Set the bottles up in a row, and have the child roll the ball toward the "pins."

Ask the child to identify the letter on each pin he or she knocks down. If the child identifies the letter correctly, the pin stays knocked down. If the child cannot identify the letter, the pin is set back up. Continue playing until all pins have been knocked down and all letters correctly identified.

WHAT IS THE LETTER?

Give a child a "feel" for the letters of the alphabet.

Another way for a child to experience letters is for you to "write" a letter on the child's back by slowly tracing it with your finger. Capital letters are probably the easiest to identify. Ask the child to guess the letter. He or she will have to concentrate on your motions and strokes to determine the correct letter. For an advanced child, spell out simple, three-letter words. Have the child guess the three letters and, if possible, determine the word.

SAY A WORD

▼▼

Spin the arrow, and learn to say a new word.

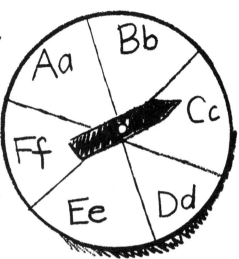

What You'll Need: Lightweight cardboard, marker or pen, compass, ruler, blunt scissors, brad fastener

Use a compass to draw a circle 8″ in diameter on a piece of cardboard. Then draw lines to divide the circle into six equal sections. At the center point of the circle, make a small hole with the scissors. Cut out a simple arrow about 3″ long and 1″ wide from another piece of cardboard to use as the spinner. Put a brad fastener through the middle of the arrow and the center of the wheel. Next, write the capital and lowercase forms of a single letter in each of the six sections of the circle. The child spins the arrow on the wheel and says a word that begins with the letter in the section where the arrow comes to rest.

Variation: To make this activity more challenging, increase the number of sections. For the child who can read, in addition to saying a word beginning with a particular letter, the child should also spell the word.

ABC CONCENTRATION

▼▼

Alike or different? Let kids decide in this game.

What You'll Need: Ten letter cards

Recognizing whether two letters are alike or different is an important reading skill. Shuffle ten letter cards (five pairs of matching letters), and lay them out faceup in two rows. Invite the child to put the five pairs of matching letters together.

Variation: Make one set of matching letters uppercase, the other set lowercase. You can also increase the number of cards used.

EYE TO HAND

ABC GO!

Kids need quick hands and sharp eyes to play this fast-paced game.

What You'll Need: Pad of self-adhesive notes, marker or pen

This activity is designed to sharpen a child's letter- and word-recognition skills.

Start with eight notes. Select four simple words, writing each one on two separate notes. Words to start with are *car, big, top,* and *nut.*

Give the child one set of words, and keep the other set. Both you and the child should attach one note to the front of each hand and one note to the back of each hand. You and the child can begin playing by putting your hands at your sides. You say, "ABC Go!" and both of you display the front or back of your right or left hand. The child looks at the words displayed by both of you and decides whether they match. If they do, the words are removed. If they do not, the game is repeated.

Play until all notes have been paired and removed. Then new words can be written. Children with more highly developed coordination can put notes on index fingers and thumbs.

LETTER WINDOWS

Open your window to see a letter, and then match it with a letter card.

What You'll Need: Poster board, light-colored construction paper, blunt scissors, glue, letter cards, pencil

Children can improve their small-muscle coordination by helping cut and paste the pieces for this activity.

Have the child help you make a house by gluing a sheet of light-colored construction paper to the poster board; this is the basic house. Make a triangular roof out of another sheet of construction paper, and glue it on top of the house shape. Draw three rows of square windows on the house, with three windows in each row. From another sheet of construction paper, cut squares the size of the house windows plus a ½" flap on top. Put glue on the flaps, and glue one over each window. With a pencil, write a letter on each window (not each flap).

After the child has studied the letters on the windows, cover each one with its flap. Remove the letter cards for the nine letters you wrote on the windows, and shuffle the nine cards. Have the child pick a card and then try to choose the window with the matching letter. If the child chooses correctly, he or she puts the letter card aside. If not, the child puts the card at the bottom of the card pile and goes on to the next letter card. Continue until all the letters have been correctly chosen. To play again, erase the letters on the windows and write new ones.

PHONICS FUN FACT
Since 1972, the *Supplement to the Oxford English Dictionary* has included more than 60,000 words.

WOOD SANDING

▼▼▼▼▼▼▼▼▼▼▼▼▼▼▼▼▼▼▼▼▼▼▼▼▼▼▼▼▼▼▼▼▼▼▼▼▼▼

Keep young hands busy going around and around, up and down, and side to side sanding wood.

What You'll Need: Wood, sandpaper

Need some help refinishing a project? Ask the child to help you, and at the same time help the child to develop the small muscles necessary for writing.

Select a piece of wood. Give the child a piece of coarse sandpaper. Show the child how to sand the furniture by using different motions—circular, up and down, and back and forth. Describe these motions as they are being done. These are the same motions that are used when writing letters.

ALPHABET MEASURING

▼▼▼▼▼▼▼▼▼▼▼▼▼▼▼▼▼▼▼▼▼▼▼▼▼▼▼▼▼▼▼▼▼▼▼▼▼▼

Mix one measure of counting with two measures of letter identification.

What You'll Need: Measuring spoon, small container of sand (or flour), plastic knife, three plastic drinking cups (marked *A, B,* and *C*)

Following your specific instructions, a child can master measuring skills while learning to recognize letters.

Show the child how to dip the measuring spoon into the sand (or flour), level it with a plastic knife, and pour it into a cup. Have the child follow your directions and put specific amounts of sand in the letter cups. For example, you might say, "Put two tablespoons of sand in the *B* cup," or, "Put three tablespoons of sand in the *C* cup." For an added challenge, add more letter cups.

CHANGE IT!

▼▼

Sneaky things can happen in this alphabet memory game.

What You'll Need: Set of letter cards

Memory games can help children develop the visualization skills essential to reading.

Shuffle the cards, and lay down three cards in a row faceup. Have the child study the cards so that he or she will remember them. Ask the child to turn around, then add one card or take one away. Ask him or her to turn back around and tell you what has changed. As the child becomes more adept at the game, make more complex changes, such as replacing one card with another.

DIGIT LETTERS

▼▼

What letters can you make with your fingers?

Making letters with your fingers can be fun, yet challenging. It can also help a child who is having difficulty distinguishing between similar letters—lowercase *b* and *d,* for example.

With your left hand, use the middle finger, pointer finger, and thumb to form what will look like the signal for "okay": The pointer finger and thumb form a circle, then line up the rest of the fingers straight in a single row. When you have done that, a lowercase *b* has been made. Do the same finger formations with your right hand to make a lowercase *d.*

If you place these two letter formations side by side, they look like a bed with two pillows. Seeing this, the child can then associate the beginning sound *b* and the ending sound *d* in the word *bed.* This helps him or her remember the differences between the two letters, and it reinforces the process of reading from left to right. See how many other finger letters the child can make.

ABC STAR

▼▼▼▼▼▼▼▼▼▼▼▼▼▼▼▼▼▼▼▼▼▼▼▼▼▼▼▼▼▼▼▼▼▼▼▼

Follow the letter dots, and see what shines.

What You'll Need: Follow-the-dot picture, pencil, tissue paper, paper

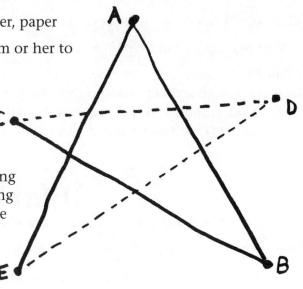

To help a child learn the sequence of the alphabet, ask him or her to connect a series of dots to form a picture.

The child will have to draw a line from letters *A* to *B*, *B* to *C*, and so on until an object appears. As the child masters the alphabet, the pictures can be made more complex.

Start by drawing (or tracing) a simple, easily recognizable object on a sheet of tissue paper. Transfer this image by placing the tissue paper on top of a regular sheet of paper and pressing dots along the object's outline at regular intervals. Mark these dots on the paper with a sequence of letters beginning with *A*, and have the child connect the dots by following the sequence of the alphabet.

PHONICS FUN FACT
No other language has more words spelled similarly, but pronounced differently than English. Consider: *heard—beard, low—how, paid—said, break—speak, five—give, four—tour,* and *ache—mustache.*

GIVE ME A RING

This ringtoss game makes it fun to practice one of the more difficult letters.

What You'll Need: Poster board or lightweight cardboard, blunt scissors, compass, 12″ to 24″ tall pole, paper, pen

Active children can prepare to write by playing all kinds of physical games.

To make a ringtoss game, cut several rings from poster board or cardboard. Make the hole of each ring about 6″ in diameter. Put the pole in clay or sand to hold it upright. Invite the child to throw the rings around the pole. Each time he or she succeeds, have the child say the word *ring* and write the letter *R* on a scorecard. Continue until the child has scored at least five rings.

PENCIL, CRAYON, MARKER

Here's an activity that exercises hands and minds.

What You'll Need: Paper, pencil, crayon, marker

Writing with three different instruments will give children plenty of hand exercise.

In a row at the top of a sheet of paper, draw a small pencil, a crayon, and a marker. Write the letter *P* next to the pencil, *C* next to the crayon, and *M* next to the marker. Make up a sentence that contains a word that begins with *P, C,* or *M.* For example, you might say, "I went to the store, and I saw *potatoes* (or *crackers* or *milk*)." Ask the child to use the writing tool whose name has the same beginning letter as the word to write that word in the correct column. (You may need to help the child spell the word.)

DIALING FINGERS

Children who are itching to use the phone like grown-ups will be satisfied with this pretend activity.

What You'll Need: Pen or pencil, paper, toy telephone with push buttons containing letters

Here's a spelling exercise that introduces a child to one of the wonders of modern technology: the telephone.

Explain to the child that, with real telephones, people must use specific numbers when they want to call someone. Tell the child that you will play a game in which he or she pretends to call friends and relatives by pressing the letters in their names instead of telephone numbers.

Ask the child to name someone, such as "David," who he or she will pretend to phone. Print the name on a piece of paper. Have the child say the letter that stands for the beginning sound in the name and then press the button on the phone that has that letter.

See if he or she can finish spelling the name this way. If not, you can help by saying the letter and having the child find and press the correct button on the telephone.

PHONICS FUN FACT
Of the 20,000 common words containing the consonant *f*, only in the word *of* is the *f* pronounced irregularly (that is, like a *v* instead of an *f*).

ABC CUPS

▼▼

It's sort of satisfying to put objects into their very own letter cups.

What You'll Need: Permanent marker, masking tape, three plastic drinking cups, small objects as described below

What seems like a simple sorting exercise reinforces a child's vocabulary and the ability to identify letters.

Mark three plastic drinking cups with the letters *A, B,* and *C* (one letter per cup) using a permanent marker and masking tape labels. Collect several small objects whose names begin with each of these letters, such as an animal cracker, toy airplane, and an acorn for the letter *A*; a ball, bandage, and bean for the letter *B*; and a playing card, piece of candy, and a cotton ball for the letter *C*.

Put the items in random order on a table, and ask the child to put each object in the cup with its beginning letter on it. Discuss the names of the objects as the child completes the activity. Repeat the activity using other letters and objects.

STRING LETTERS

▼▼

String 'em up! Use common string to form letters.

What You'll Need: Pieces of string, paper and pen (optional)

Manipulating string requires the child to use muscles necessary for fine motor coordination.

Using different thicknesses and lengths of string, a child can form letters of the alphabet. For example, the string can be swirled into the letter *S,* or it can be zigzagged to form a *Z*. Try to describe each letter the child makes using a word that begins with that letter. For example, point out the swirling *S,* the zigzag *Z,* and the curved *C*. For younger children, it may be helpful to begin with sheets of paper that have letters already drawn on them.

WORD SENSE

A STORY TO BE TOLD

▼▼▼▼▼▼▼▼▼▼▼▼▼▼▼▼▼▼▼▼▼▼▼▼▼▼▼▼▼▼▼▼▼▼▼▼▼▼▼

Make a new story every time you "read" a picture book.

What You'll Need: Picture book, paper, pencil

A child needs to be able to interpret or "read" pictures since sight recognition of words is very limited at a young age. By looking at pictures, stories can be understood—or imagined.

Select a picture book without written text, and look at it with the child. After going through the book, ask the child if anything seemed to be missing. When the child responds that there aren't any words, suggest that you can add them and write the story together.

Ask the child to look carefully at the pictures and tell you what he or she thinks is happening. As the child is describing a picture, write his or her story on a piece of paper. Ask the child to name different beginning-letter sounds of the words in his or her story. For example, if the story involves a monkey, ask the child, "What letter does the word *monkey* begin with?" You can take this even further by asking, "What does a monkey like to eat?" When the child answers "bananas," ask him or her what letter the word *bananas* begins with.

When finished, sit back and enjoy reading the whole story with the child. A new interpretation of the pictures may be made another day.

WHAT DOES IT SAY?

Every object has a name. Match words to objects in your room.

What You'll Need: Index cards, markers

After letter sounds have been mastered and the capital and lowercase letters have been learned, the next step is to apply that knowledge to reading words.

Write simple words (for example, *ball, pen, desk, cup*) on index cards. Make sure the words correspond to objects found in the child's room. Give the child a card, and ask him or her to sound out the word printed on the card. When the word is said, instruct the child to take the card to his or her room, locate the object matching that word, and place the card next to the identified object.

TALL TALES

Weave an alphabetical tale with a group of friends.

Children can put the alphabet to good use in this group activity.

Alternating turns with one or more friends or parents, the first child names a word beginning with the letter *A*, the next person picks a word beginning with *B*, and so on. To complicate the exercise, the words should combine to tell a story. For example: *Alice Bakes Cookie Dough Every Friday.* See if you can use the entire alphabet. As the story evolves, it can be written down and read when completed.

TIC-TAC-TOE RHYMES

Tic-tac-toe, three in a row!

What You'll Need: Two sheets of drawing paper, marker or pen, crayons or coloring pencils, blunt scissors, board game markers

Here's a way to play this classic game while learning to recognize letters and rhyming words.

Make a game card by dividing a sheet of drawing paper into nine squares (three rows of three squares). Help the child draw or color the following pictures inside the squares: a hat, mouse, boy, peach, car, goose, tree, boat, and dime. Divide a second sheet of paper into nine squares. This time, the child should draw or color a cat, house, toy, beach, jar, moose, bee, coat, and lime inside the squares and then cut these squares apart with blunt scissors.

To play, shuffle the picture cards. Players take turns picking a card and matching it to a rhyming word on the game board. If a player makes a correct match, he or she puts a board game marker on the square. The first player to get three markers across, down, or on a diagonal wins the game.

PHONICS FUN FACT
The most common words in *written* English are *the, of, to, in, and, a, for, was, is,* and *that.* The most common words in *spoken* English are *the, and, I, to, of, a, you, that, in,* and *it.*

WORD TO PICTURE

Have fun matching beginning letters to selected pictures.

What You'll Need: Index cards, pen or marker, several magazines, blunt scissors, glue or clear tape

By using letter sound skills, a child can match pictures with beginning sounds.

Find pictures of things in magazines that are familiar to the child. Cut the pictures out, and glue or tape them onto index cards. Take another set of index cards, and write on them the beginning letter of each object pictured.

Put the picture cards and letter cards on a table. Have the child choose a picture card and say the name of the object. Next, have him or her look at the letter cards and select the card with the same first letter as the object in the picture. Match the two cards. Later, select the letter card first, sound it out, and then ask the child to locate the matching picture.

READ THE PAPER

Introduce the child to the local newspaper.

What You'll Need: Newspaper

This activity will make children feel grown-up as they look for words in a newspaper.

Point to a word in a newspaper headline, and ask the child to find the same word somewhere else on the page. If necessary, point to the story or paragraph in which the word can be found. To begin, find proper names since words that begin with capital letters are easier to spot. For a bigger challenge, help the child read the words that he or she finds.

WORD HANG-UP

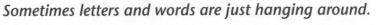

Sometimes letters and words are just hanging around.

What You'll Need: Paper, old magazines, blunt scissors, letter cards, marker or pen, clothes hanger, plastic clothespins

Help children enjoy unusual methods of putting letters together to make words in this activity.

Think of several easy words, such as *dog, cat, bird, car, jet, cup, pig,* and *boy.* While searching through old magazines, find and cut out a picture of each one. Put a clothes hanger on a doorknob. Display the first picture. Instruct the child to find the letter cards that spell the word and clip them onto the hanger with clothespins.

COPYCAT WORDS

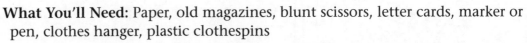

Copycat or oddball? Kids decide as they look at and listen to a series of words.

What You'll Need: Paper, pen

In this activity, children recognize both visually and aurally whether words are the same or different.

On a sheet of paper, write a series of three words, such as *cat/can/cat.* Read the words aloud. Ask the child to circle the word that is different. Write another row of words without reading them aloud. Again, have the child circle the word that looks different. Read the words, and ask the child to repeat them. Continue with other series of words, such as *pig/pig/big; dog/hog/dog; bed/red/red; pink/pink/sink; hen/ten/ten;* and *five/five/dive.*

REBUS WRITING

▼▼

Have fun writing and reading picture stories.

What You'll Need: Magazines, blunt scissors, paper, glue or clear tape, pencil

As the child's ability to read improves, try a rebus story. A rebus story combines written words with pictures of familiar objects.

Have the child pick a topic to write about—perhaps a day at the beach. The child will say the words he or she knows and—with your help—write them down. A picture cut from a magazine is used in place of writing when the child comes to a difficult word. For example:

I went to the (picture of a beach).

I saw (picture of seashells).

I made a (picture of a sandcastle).

I had fun.

Remind the child what type of letter is at the beginning of a sentence (capital letter) and what goes at the end of a sentence (usually a period, question mark, or exclamation point). When the story is complete, ask the child to read it back to you.

PHONICS FUN FACT
The letter of the alphabet with the highest frequency of use is *e*. The most frequent initial letter is *s*. The least commonly used initial letters are *q, x, y,* and *z*.

SIGN SYMBOLS

Signs are everywhere. While traveling, identify and interpret these signs and symbols.

Next time you take an automobile trip to visit grandparents or friends, ask the child to look for traffic and advertising signs and symbols and tell you what they are. Early reading begins by interpreting various signs and symbols and associating words, sounds, and meanings to them.

One of the first signs that usually is recognized is the hexagonal STOP sign. Also look for ONE WAY, SCHOOL ZONE, NO CROSSING, and other signs and symbols during your trip. This activity expands the child's reading environment and encourages the use of beginning sounds.

READ THE LABEL

Take a closer look at the words that are part of our everyday life.

What You'll Need: Index cards, marker or pen, clear tape

In this activity, children learn to recognize the words that name objects they see every day.

Make word cards with the names of objects in a room. For example, in the kitchen, you might write the words *chair, table, sink, floor,* and *window.* Help the child match each card with the object it names and tape the card to the object. Have the child walk around the room and "read" the label on each object. Try other rooms, such as the bedroom *(bed, desk, lamp, closet)* and living room *(couch, chair, TV, shelf).*

WORD DOMINOES

Word matching is fun when it's done with dominoes.

What You'll Need: Index cards, marker or pen

Playing a domino game gives children practice in visually matching words.

Make ten word dominoes by placing each card horizontally and drawing a vertical line down the center. Write a simple word on either side of the line. Write each word on two different cards. Also, make cards that have the same word twice. For example, a set of cards might read *cat/dog, dog/pig, pig/ball, ball/run, run/cat, cat/cat, dog/dog, pig/pig, ball/ball,* and *run/run.*

Play the game by spreading out the cards facedown. Take turns picking a card and placing it with one end or the other next to a card with a matching word. If you select a card that doesn't match any of the words displayed, put it on the bottom of the pile and select another card. Eventually, all of the cards should be connected.

RHYMES FROM A TO Z

Z *is for* Zoo—*and that rhymes with* boo, too, *and* moo!

Combine rhyming skills with a review of the alphabet and beginning sounds in this game.

Display the alphabet. Point to the letter *A* and say, "*A* is for *and.*" The child must name a rhyming word *(band, hand, land, sand)*. Continue with *B* is for *ball, C* is for *cat, D* is for *dig,* and so on. Challenge a more advanced child by having him or her give a letter and a word while you say a rhyme.

SOCCER IS A KICK

Young children can play an educational version of their big sisters' and brothers' favorite game.

What You'll Need: Marker, kraft paper, yardstick, removable tape, soccer ball or large ball that bounces

In this activity, children can practice their soccer skills—and learn a new word.

Make a soccer "goal" by writing the word *kick* with a marker in large letters on a piece of kraft paper measuring at least three feet by three feet. Tape the sign on a wall in a gym, basement, or recreation room.

Ask the child to identify the initial letter in the word and its beginning sound. Say the word, and have the child demonstrate the action of kicking the ball. Tell the child to stand several feet back from the *kick* sign and kick the ball toward it. Each time he or she hits the "goal," the child can shout a word that begins with the same sound as *kick!*

LETTER SCRAMBLE

Spell a word—sound by sound and letter by letter.

What You'll Need: Index cards, pen or marker, picture cards

When the child has learned all of the capital and lowercase letters of the alphabet, you can help him or her take the next step in language development.

Show the child a picture card (for example, a hat), then give him or her a stack of randomly mixed index cards, each one containing one of the letters required to spell the pictured object (in this case, *T, H,* and *A*). First, have the child tell you what the object in the picture is. Then sound out each letter in the word, and have the child take the corresponding letter card and place it in the proper spelling order. Have the child say the word and spell it aloud. Continue in this manner with other picture cards.

ALL ABOUT ME

Be an author! Here's a chance to write an autobiography.

What You'll Need: Crayons, paper, yarn or O-rings, hole puncher

What better way for a child to express himself or herself than by writing a book?

Ask the child to draw a picture of himself or herself and write his or her name below the picture. Other pages to be added to the book may be about family, friends, favorite foods, toys, books, colors, or places to visit. When the child has drawn these pictures, write a caption sentence about each page; for example, "My favorite food is _____." Say the letters as you are writing so the child associates them with their sounds.

Help the child make a special cover for this book. Assemble the book by punching holes along one side of each page. Yarn or O-rings can then be used to bind the book. On the back cover, date the book. It will become a keepsake. Try making a new book every month or two to see how the child's ideas, art, and spelling ability change from one time to the next.

PHONICS FUN FACT

Although there are about 40 different sounds in English, there are more than 200 ways of spelling them. The long O sound can be spelled in several ways: *stow, though, doe, sew, soul,* and *beau.* The long A sound can be spelled as in *rate, main, stay, paid, freight, break, veil, ballet,* and *obey.* The SH sound can be spelled in the following ways: *shoe, sugar, special, passion, delicious, ocean, tissue, conscience, nation,* and *champagne.*

ZOO

▼▼

Every child likes to act like an animal sometimes, and this game actively encourages it.

What You'll Need: Sheet of paper, marker or pen

Children's natural love of animals can be channeled into wordplay that helps develop reading skills.

On a sheet of paper, print the word *ZOO* in capital letters. Ask the child to identify the first letter of the word. Say the word together several times.

Talk with the child about trips to the zoo or about zoos he or she may have seen on TV or in movies, and encourage the child to think about some of the animals he or she saw there. Whenever the child mentions a specific animal, ask him or her to identify the beginning letter of the animal's name. Make a list of all the animals the child names, then show him or her the list and say, "Can you find the _____?" Read one of the animal names on the list, and see if the child can find that word.

Variation: Take turns acting like zoo animals, such as an elephant, monkey, gorilla, lion, and bear, as the other player guesses the animal's identity and identifies the word on the list.

ALPHABET COOKING

SOFT PRETZEL LETTERS

Twist some dough to make letters—and pretzels.

What You'll Need: Measuring cups, water, sugar, salt, one packet yeast, mixing bowl, big spoon, flour, baking sheet, aluminum foil, egg, pastry brush, kosher salt, pot holder

Measuring, stirring, mixing, and kneading are the procedures the child will use to make soft pretzels. These tasks can be fun for a child, and the result will be something that he or she will enjoy eating.

With the child's help, measure 1½ cups of warm water, one tablespoon of sugar, one teaspoon of salt, and one packet of yeast. Ask the child to pour the ingredients into a mixing bowl and stir. Add four cups of flour to the other ingredients, and mix thoroughly. The child can remove the dough from the bowl and knead it on a floured tabletop. The child will use all of his or her hand and finger muscles to knead the dough until it is smooth. As the child is kneading the dough, discuss the different possible types of pretzel shapes you could make.

When the kneading is completed, pull off a piece of dough and shape it to make several letters (perhaps the initials of the child's name). Place these shapes on a baking sheet lined with aluminum foil. Brush the pretzel letters with a beaten egg, and sprinkle with coarse kosher salt. Bake the letters at 425 degrees for 12 to 15 minutes or until they are golden brown. Let cool before eating.

Exercise proper safety around the oven. Do not allow the child to come in contact with the heated baking sheet.

FRUITFUL FUN

▼▼

Children learn the names of fruits in this mouth-watering activity.

What You'll Need: Various fruits, package of fruit string (available at grocery stores)

In this activity, children review fruit names as they work on beginning letters.

Name a fruit, such as an apple, and hold up a real apple. Have the child form the fruit string into the shape of the letter *A* for the word's beginning sound. Take turns naming other fruits, such as a banana, peach, pear, watermelon, apricot, cantaloupe, nectarine, orange, and berries. Start with common fruits, and hold up examples of each. For an added challenge, have the child describe each fruit as it is named or give clues for each fruit instead of naming it.

SWEET OR SOUR?

▼▼

Kids must get their taste buds working for this savory experience.

What You'll Need: Snack foods as described below

Show your good taste as you help a child review words that begin with the letter *S*.

Have the child taste several different food items and describe their tastes with an *S* word. Explain that many different kinds of tastes can be described with *S* words, such as *sweet, sour, spicy, salty, sticky,* and *sugary.* The word *soft* can also describe foods.

Prepare some snacks from among the following: potato chips, dill pickle, sweet pickle, salsa, bread with peanut butter, pretzel, bread with jelly, hot dog, or salami. The child can also taste lemon juice and other juices. Have the child taste each food and use one or more *S* words to describe it.

PUDDING PAINT

Here's a way to write that's a little messy, but delicious.

What You'll Need: Instant pudding mix, milk, mixer, bowl, big spoon, plastic plates

What child can resist an activity that encourages putting his or her fingers in food?

Stress the importance of clean hands when working with food items. Then have the child help you mix a package of instant pudding. (Chocolate or another dark pudding works well.) Read the directions, and discuss each step. Spread a layer of pudding on a large plastic plate. Show the child how to finger-paint in the pudding. Name several letters for the child to write, or write some on paper for him or her to copy. The child may also wish to write his or her name.

SOUND SUPERMARKET

Cans of food can be useful for teaching beginning sounds.

What You'll Need: Canned goods, grocery bag

Children love to pretend, and they love to go grocery shopping. Combine both activities. This game also reinforces children's recognition of beginning sounds.

Put several cans of food on a table. Explain to the child that he or she is going to pretend to go grocery shopping. In order to "buy" a food, the child must say a word that begins with the same sound as the name of the food (for example, *carrots/coin, soup/sun, beans/ball*). Have the child choose a can and then name the food it contains. After he or she says a word with the same beginning sound as the food name, the child puts the food into the grocery bag.

At the end of the game, have the child count the cans to see how many groceries he or she has "bought." As the cans are taken out of the bag, ask him or her to say the beginning sound of the food item.

THAT'S CHEESY!

You can eat the letters in this tasty alphabet game.

What You'll Need: American cheese slices or block of cheese, knife, ruler

In this activity, children can make letters out of cheese strips or sticks.

Cut slices of American cheese into strips, or slice a block of any firm cheese such as mild cheddar, mozzarella, or Monterey Jack into sticks. (Be careful with the knife around the child.) Make the sticks approximately 2 inches long and ½ inch wide. Have the child wash his or her hands, then show him or her how to form the cheese sticks into letters. Start with letters that are easier to form, such as *E, F, H,* and *L.* Have the child form and identify several letters before eating them.

PHONICS FUN FACT
A syllable is a word or part of a word pronounced with a single vocal sound. Each syllable must have a vowel, but not necessarily a consonant.

MAKE A MENU

What goes with chicken and chili? In this game, cheddar cheese.

What You'll Need: Seven paper plates, canned goods, old magazines, blunt scissors, marker or pen

This activity allows children to help plan lunch menus as they review beginning sounds.

Put seven paper plates in a row. Write a day of the week on each plate. Invite the child to help you plan a week's worth of lunch menus by planning each day's menu around a different beginning sound. To illustrate each menu, have the child find canned goods and boxed goods in the kitchen, or find and cut out pictures of food. For example, you might start with the beginning sound *M* (macaroni, meat, milk). The child might find a box of macaroni and cheese and cut out a picture of a glass of milk. Other menu letters could be *S* (soup, sandwich), *T* (tuna, toast, tomatoes), *P* (peanut butter, pear, potato salad), *H* (hot dog, hamburger), *B* (banana, beans), and *F* (fish, French fries).

FAVORITE FOOD FILE

Get your recipe file in order (alphabetical order) in this activity.

What You'll Need: Index cards, pen or pencil

Use an alphabetical theme to make a recipe file of the child's favorite foods.

Start by asking the child, "What's your favorite food that starts with *P*?" Write a recipe card for the child's response. Point out the name of the recipe (for example, "Pepperoni Pizza"), and then discuss the steps of the recipe as you write them. Some children may wish to point out the letter *P* wherever it appears in the recipe. Continue with other letters such as *B, H, S, T,* and *M*.

ALPHABET SALAD

If you've never had a radish and jalapeño pepper salad, try this recipe.

What You'll Need: Letter cards containing the letters *A* through *T,* box or bowl, various vegetables, pen or pencil, paper

This activity tests a child's memory as well as his or her vocabulary.

Put the letter cards in a box or bowl, and mix them up. Ask the child to choose seven letters and name each one. Then have him or her name vegetables that could be put into a salad whose name begins with each letter. Point out that some letters may have several items and others may have none. You can also help name items for difficult letters.

Keep the following ingredients in mind: asparagus, avocado, beans, broccoli, cabbage, carrots, celery, cucumber, garlic, green pepper, jalapeño pepper, lettuce, mushrooms, olives, onions, parsley, peas, radish, red pepper, spinach, and tomato. You may also suggest other salad items, such as apples, eggs, and nuts.

Write down each vegetable the child names. Edit the list together, choosing several items for a real salad. Shop for the items together. Discuss each vegetable as you prepare it and add it to the salad.

ALPHABET ARTS & CRAFTS

LETTER NECKLACE

Help kids make a simple necklace they can wear with pride.

What You'll Need: Index cards, marker or pen, old magazines (optional), blunt scissors (optional), glue or clear tape (optional), hole puncher, 24″ length of yarn, paper clip

In this activity, children can show what they've learned by wearing it around their necks.

Use three to four index cards. On the first card, write a letter. On each of the other cards, the child should draw a picture of an item whose name begins with that letter. Or you can ask the child to cut out magazine pictures of objects that have the same first letter and glue or tape them on the cards.

When the child has completed the cards, punch two holes at the top of each one. String the yarn through the cards, keeping the letter card in the center. Have the child name the letter and the pictured items. Put the stringed cards around the child's neck so he or she can wear them like a necklace. Fasten the ends fairly loosely with a paper clip (to prevent a choking hazard).

LETTER HEADBAND

▼▼

Stylish kids will enjoy making wearable art with letters.

What You'll Need: Construction paper, blunt scissors, stapler, pen or pencil, crayons or colored markers, glue or clear tape

In this activity, the alphabet goes to children's heads!

Cut a long strip of construction paper about 2″ wide. Put the strip around the child's head. Find a comfortable fit for the headband, and staple the ends of the band together.

On sheets of construction paper, draw outlines of letters and have the child color them in. Discuss the names of the letters as he or she colors. You may want to focus on one letter or on several letters. Cut out the letters, and help the child glue or tape them onto the headband. The child can wear the headband or take it off and name the letters.

SOUND STAGE

▼▼

Set the stage for fun by designing a diorama.

What You'll Need: Shoe box, crayons, construction paper, blunt scissors, glue, found objects

Challenge a child's creativity by making a diorama that illustrates a beginning sound.

First, discuss with the child a possible theme for a diorama based on a single beginning sound—such as "Patsy Petunia's Palace," "Timmy Turtle's Tree," or "Sandy's Sports Store."

Turn the shoe box on its side, and show the child how to decorate the floor, ceiling, and walls of the diorama with crayons and construction paper. Then have the child make or collect objects for the diorama that start with the same beginning sound. For example, "Patsy Petunia's Palace" could contain Patsy, a petunia, a pig, a picture, and pots and pans. Use your imagination!

SHAPE WIND CHIMES

▼▼

Hear lovely sounds when the wind blows these "chimes."

What You'll Need: Clay, waxed paper, rolling pin, plastic knife, pencil, string, 6″ dowel rod or stick

Small hand muscles will be used as the child kneads and squeezes clay to make it pliable.

Give the child a ball of clay to knead and soften. As he or she is squeezing and "working" the clay (on a piece of waxed paper), ask him or her, "How does it feel, and what shape does it have?" Look around the room to find other shapes (for example, a rectangle, square, triangle, and diamond). Talk about them, and identify their beginning-letter sounds (the letter *R* for rectangle, *S* for square, and so on).

When the clay is softened, have the child roll it with a rolling pin to make it flat. Help him or her cut out shapes from the clay with a plastic knife. Give directions as follows: "Make a shape that begins with an *R*." Continue with the other beginning letters *(T, S, D)* to create different shapes.

Carefully lift the clay shapes, and put them on another sheet of waxed paper. Take a pencil, and make a hole at the top of each shape. When the clay is thoroughly dry, ask the child to help you tie one end of the string to each shape (through each hole) and the other end of the string to a stick or dowel rod. Tie another piece of string to the rod so the shapes can be hung as wind "chimes."

As you and the child are hanging these chimes where the wind can blow them, ask him or her to name the *W* word that causes the chimes to make sounds. (Answer: *wind*.) Review the beginning sounds of the suspended shapes.

SURF'S UP!

▼▼▼

A smart whale can help alphabet surfers challenge the waves.

What You'll Need: Large sheet of art paper, crayons or colored markers (including blue), piece of gray poster board, blunt scissors, glue or clear tape, craft stick

Here's a whale of a game that makes identifying letters fun.

On a large sheet of paper, draw ocean waves. Make at least 10 wave peaks. At the top of each wave peak, write a letter. Have the child color the ocean blue. Next, ask the child to draw the outline of a whale on a piece of gray poster board. Cut it out, and glue or tape the whale to a craft stick.

To play the game, ask the child to make the whale travel over the waves. In order to go from one wave to the next, the child must identify the letter on the wave. If the child misses a letter, he or she must go back to the beginning.

PHONICS FUN FACT
The letter *y* can be either a consonant or a vowel. In *year*, it's a consonant. In *happy*, it's a vowel.

LETTER MOBILE

Collect two- and three-dimensional items for this mobile display.

What You'll Need: Construction paper, pen or marker, blunt scissors, hole puncher, string or yarn, wire coat hanger, old magazines, collected items (see below)

A mobile is an interesting way to display a letter. Have the child choose a letter. Draw it on construction paper, and cut it out. Punch a small hole in the top, attach a piece of yarn or string, and hang it from the hanger.

Have the child collect pictures and other items whose names begin with the same letter. For example, choosing the letter *C*, the child might find a paper cup, a cookie cutter, and a picture of a cat. Hang the items on the mobile with string or yarn of varying lengths.

GOOEY DOUGH

Half the fun of this letter activity is mixing up the dough.

What You'll Need: Ingredients for Gooey Dough (see below), plastic bag

Children can make three-dimensional letters with this homemade modeling dough.

Mix two cups of salt and ⅔ cup of water. Heat until almost boiling. In a separate bowl, mix one cup of cornstarch and ½ cup of cold water. Pour it into the hot salt-and-water mixture. Let it cool.

Say words, and have the child use the Gooey Dough to shape letters that stand for the beginning sounds. The child can work with the dough on a kitchen counter or a plastic surface. Store the dough in a plastic bag to reuse it.

WHAT'S IN A NAME?

Here's an art project that adds a new dimension to letter shapes.

What You'll Need: Markers, construction paper or poster board, paints, bits of fabric, glue

Children will enjoy decorating their own and others' names with many colors and textures.

Start with the child's name. Write it in large, outlined letters on a sheet of construction paper or poster board. Brainstorm with the child to come up with different ways to decorate each letter (for example, with pictures and designs made with paint or markers, or perhaps with cut-up bits of fabric glued to the paper).

After doing his or her own name, have the child make decorative names for friends and family members. Encourage the child to personalize the decoration by using pictures, designs, and colors that remind him or her of each person.

 # FINGER PAINT DESIGNS

Try your hand at finger painting, and see what you can make.

What You'll Need: Finger paint, paper

Set up some finger paints, and have the child experiment with different hand and finger motions, such as making swirls, straight lines, curved lines, zigzag lines, circles, half circles, and spirals. These motions mirror the ones that will be needed for writing.

SOCK PUPPETS

Have one unmatched sock left over when your laundry is done? Put that lonely sock to use.

What You'll Need: Clean sock, yarn, scraps of fabric, blunt scissors, marker, buttons, cardboard, glue

Have you ever finished the laundry and found that you had only one sock? What can you do with one sock?

Give it to a child, and help him or her make a sock puppet. Ask the child to think about what kind of puppet character he or she wants. Using different scraps of yarn and fabric, help the child cut out hair, scarves, a tie, or whatever is required for this special puppet. A marker or buttons can be used to make the eyes. Place a narrow strip of cardboard inside the sock before gluing objects to it. This prevents the glue from seeping through to the inside.

After the puppet is finished and the glue has dried, have a puppet show. Oral communication is very important in a young child's language development. For children who are shy, this provides an opportunity to speak through another object.

ALPHABET ILLUSTRATION

Alphabet art lets young illustrators stretch their creative muscles.

What You'll Need: Washable paints, paintbrush, paper

This activity is a great way to reinforce the idea of beginning letters.

Suggest a letter, and explain to the child that he or she should paint a picture that contains items whose names begin with the letter. For example, an *S* picture might contain a sun, sand, a sea, a sidewalk, and a sailboat. A letter *B* picture might contain a bus, building, bird, balloon, and bench. When the child completes the picture, encourage him or her to point out each item with the chosen letter.

PEEK-A-BOO WINDOWS

▼▼

Open windows of opportunity to practice beginning sounds.

What You'll Need: Construction paper, marker or pen, blunt scissors, drawing paper

In this activity, children create windows that they can open to identify the pictures inside and make their beginning sounds.

Fold a sheet of construction paper in half, from top to bottom. On one half, draw two large squares. Cut three sides of each square, and fold the paper back to form a flap. Fold a sheet of drawing paper in half, also from top to bottom. Make a "book" by folding the construction paper, flap side on top, over the drawing paper.

Mark the positions of the construction-paper squares on the drawing paper. Set the construction-paper cover aside. Ask the child to draw a picture of an object in each square on the drawing paper. Put the construction-paper cover back on the paper. Ask the child to open each flap and identify the object in each window, along with the object's beginning sound. Continue by creating new pages of pictures to put inside the construction-paper cover.

TV STAR

▼▼

Acting out a favorite nursery rhyme is even more fun "on-screen."

What You'll Need: Large cardboard box, scissors or knife, crayons

Reinforce children's enjoyment of rhyme as they star on their own television screen.

Find a very large box such as one used for a large appliance. Cut a large square hole in one side of the box (keep the scissors or knife out of the reach of the child). Have the child decorate the "television" with knobs and controls. Then have the child recite and act out a nursery rhyme on the TV screen—that is, from inside the box.

The child may choose to be a character from such rhymes as "Mary, Mary, Quite Contrary," "Little Jack Horner," "Mary Had a Little Lamb," or "Jack and Jill."

CLAY PLAY DAY

Every child is a sculptor in this easy letter-formation activity.

What You'll Need: Clay or homemade modeling dough (see recipe below), plastic bag, plastic knife (optional), paper, marker or pen

Forming three-dimensional letters allows children to experience the alphabet with their sense of touch as well as sight.

To make claylike dough at home, heat a mixture of 1½ cups of water and 1½ cups of salt until it is almost boiling. Remove the mixture from the heat. Add two tablespoons of salad oil and two tablespoons powdered alum (available in the spice aisle in the supermarket). Cool the mixture for five minutes. Work in two to three cups of flour with your hands. The dough can be stored in plastic bags at room temperature and can be used for about a month.

Show the child how to roll small balls of clay into coils about six inches long. Or you may choose to cut strips from a flat sheet of clay. Write a letter on a sheet of paper. Have the child form the letter with clay strips. Start with simple letters, such as *T* and *L*, and continue with more complex letters, such as *A* and *B*.

ALPHABET ADVENTURES

STEPPING STONES

▼▼

Practicing beginning sounds can sometimes become a balancing act.

What You'll Need: Large, flat stones; letter cards made from index cards

In this activity, children improve balance and dexterity as they practice beginning sounds outdoors.

In the yard or a park, find several large, flat stones and arrange them into a path. (Or you can find an existing stone path.) Make sure the child can step from one stone to the next without difficulty.

Put a different letter card on or beside each stone. Tell the child that in order to step on each stone, he or she must say a word that begins with the sound the letter stands for. If the child gives an incorrect answer, he or she must return to the beginning of the stone path.

LETTER LION

▼▼

Make friends with a lion that only eats letters.

What You'll Need: Large sheet of brown wrapping paper, marker or pen, blunt scissors, box, letter cards made from index cards

Younger children will enjoy practicing beginning sounds by feeding a hungry lion.

On brown wrapping paper, draw a large lion's head. Cut a large, round hole for a mouth. Put the lion's head on a box with a hole cut in the position of the lion's mouth. You might also hang the lion on a door. In order to feed the lion, the child must take a letter card, identify the letter, and say a word that begins with the sound the letter stands for. If the child gives correct answers, he or she drops the card into the lion's mouth.

BOX BOUNCE

▼▼

Here's a game that tests coordination and quickness—both mental and physical.

What You'll Need: Small box, rubber ball

Play a ball game that will keep children active and improve their coordination while they learn letters and beginning sounds.

Show the child how to catch the ball using the box. Bounce the ball for the child to catch in the box. If he or she catches it, the child must say a word that begins with the letter *A*. When the child catches the ball a second time, he or she must say a word beginning with *B*. Continue through the rest of the alphabet.

ALPHABETICAL SHOPPING

From apples to zucchini, the grocery store has everything. What can you find?

What You'll Need: Paper, pen or pencil

Try this alphabetical shopping activity. It may take some extra time.

Before going grocery shopping, ask the child to help you put your shopping list in alphabetical order. If the list is short and you don't mind doing a little extra walking, locate the items in the store in alphabetical order.

If your shopping list is long, shop as you normally do, but let the child cross off each item from the list as you locate it.

COMICAL COMICS

Kids can have fun with phonics by focusing on the funnies.

What You'll Need: Comic strip from newspaper, blunt scissors

Reading the comics is a great way to introduce children to newspapers.

Read several comic strips with the child. Point out simple words as you read. Have the child choose a favorite strip and tell it in his or her own words. Then cut out the strip, and cut the strip into its parts. Mix the pieces up. Have the child arrange the pieces in order and tell the story. Don't worry if the pieces are not in their original order, as long as the child tells the story in a logical way.

CLIMB EVERY MOUNTAIN

See who's king of the mountain when it comes to beginning sounds.

What You'll Need: Index cards, marker or pen, blankets, cushions and pillows

Give active children a goal to reach as they practice beginning sounds.

First, make letter cards by printing letters on index cards. Make a "mountain" by stacking blankets in a big mound on the floor. You may put cushions and pillows in the center of the mound to support the mountain. Put letter cards in folds of the blankets all the way up and around the mountain. Challenge the child to climb the mountain by identifying each letter on the way to the top and saying a word that begins with that letter's sound.

As children become better at identifying the letters and sounds, have them start over at the bottom if they give an incorrect answer. If you have a real hill or something else that can be climbed in your backyard, try this activity outside.

ALPHABET CATEGORIES

Pick a category, and see how many words you can come up with.

Here's a game that can be played in the car or whenever you have a few spare minutes.

Ask the child to help choose a category, such as animals, foods, or toys. The first player must name a member of the category whose name begins with the letter *A*. The next player names one whose name begins with the letter *B*, and so on.

You may need to give the child clues for some words (having several ABC picture books may be helpful). Also, explain to the child that it may be difficult or impossible to come up with words for some letters. If a child is forced to "pass" and no one else can think of a word that begins with that letter either, he or she can move on to the next letter of the alphabet.

TRAVEL TALL TALES

▼▼

"I am going to Tallahassee, and I will take a turkey to tip the taxi driver."

This game requires players to think of several different kinds of words beginning with a particular letter.

Using letter *A* words as an example, you can start the game by saying, "I am going to *Alabama,* and I will take an *ant* to *answer* questions." A player using letter *B* words might say, "I am going to *Boston,* and I will take a *bird* to *build* a *bungalow.*"

You can simplify the game by saying the sentence and stopping when the child must think of a word: "I am going to _____, and I will take a _____ to _____."

DONKEY DE-TAILS

▼▼

Pin the tail on the donkey is more than a party game when it includes letter identification.

What You'll Need: Brown wrapping paper, marker or pen, blunt scissors, construction paper, removable tape, scarf for blindfold

Make a favorite children's game a learning experience.

Draw a donkey shape on a large sheet of wrapping paper, or use a ready-made game. Cut donkey tails out of construction paper, and put a piece of tape on each tail. Print a letter on each tail.

Blindfold the child, and have him or her pin the tail on the donkey. If the child is playing alone, have him or her pin several tails on the donkey. Otherwise, have each child pin one tail on it. When all the tails are on the donkey, have the child (or children) identify the letter on each tail and say a word that begins with the sound the letter represents.

ASPARAGUS TO ZUCCHINI

▼▼

Plant an alphabet garden from asparagus to zucchini.

What You'll Need: Vegetable seeds, pots and soil (if planting indoors), tape, craft sticks, marker, paper

Planting a garden encourages a child to develop responsibility, especially if he or she agrees to water and care for the plants.

Take the child to the store to help select different vegetable seeds to plant in your garden. Ask the child, "What vegetable begins like the word *buy?*" (Answers: beans, beets, or broccoli.) Then have the child point to that vegetable's seed packet. Continue giving other beginning-sound clues for other vegetables. Purchase the seeds. If you don't have an outdoor garden, purchase some pots and soil to use for planting indoors.

On your trip home, discuss how you and the child will begin planting. Ask the child, "What vegetable did you select that begins with the letter *B?*" Use other letters, depending on which vegetables were selected.

At planting time, read the seed packet planting directions to the child, then have him or her tell you what steps are necessary for planting these seeds. After the seeds are planted, save the packet and tape or otherwise secure it to a craft stick. Have the child write the beginning letter of that vegetable on the stick with a marker, then place this stick by the planted seeds.

Make a simple chart on which the child can place an X each day that the vegetables were cared for and watered. This encourages and reinforces responsibility on the part of the child.

Good luck with the garden, and enjoy eating those special vegetables.

GO FLY A KITE

▼▼

The sky is clear. The wind is blowing. Go fly a kite on this beautiful, windy day.

What You'll Need: Kite

Next time you look out the window and see that the wind is blowing and the leaves are moving, ask the child, "What is making the leaves blow?" (Answer: wind.) Then say to the child, "I am thinking of something that needs wind to make it fly. It's a word that begins like *kitten*. What is it?" (Answer: kite.)

Get a kite, go outside, and discuss how to fly it. Say to the child, "I am thinking of something that you will need to do to lift the kite in the air. This word begins like *race*. What is it?" (Answer: run.) Talk about other beginning-letter sounds involved in kite flying, such as *T* for tail, *S* for string, and *H* for high.

Now that the child knows how to fly a kite, have him or her face into the wind, put the kite on the ground, hold the string tight, and run. In just a matter of minutes, the kite will be flying high.

SMART ART

Visiting an art museum with a child can be an enlightening experience on many different levels.

Expand a child's world—and practice beginning sounds—by visiting an art museum and studying the paintings and sculptures found there.

Select a particular gallery in the museum that you think the child would enjoy seeing. If a certain painting or sculpture attracts the child's attention, go to that piece of art. Look at it together, and have the child describe it to you. Name a letter and ask the child to identify an object in the artwork that begins with that letter. Tell the child the name of the artist who created the artwork.

When you are at home or at the library, see if you can find a book about the child's favorite artist or find a book that contains a photo of a painting the child likes, perhaps one seen at the museum.

A DAY AT THE RACES

It could be a photo finish when kids who know beginning sounds play this board game.

What You'll Need: Poster board or wrapping paper, marker or pen, letter cards made from index cards, die and markers from a board game

Try this racetrack board game to practice beginning sounds. First, draw a large oval racetrack on poster board or a large sheet of wrapping paper. Write *Start* and *Finish* at the appropriate places. Mark the track with small squares, and place a letter card in each one. Place game markers at the beginning of the track.

Players take turns rolling the die and moving their markers along the track. When a player lands on a square, he or she must identify the letter and say a word that begins with the sound the letter stands for. If the player gives an incorrect answer, he or she goes back to *Start*. Play until someone reaches the *Finish* line.

BEGINNING, MIDDLE, OR END?

Like the best stories, most words have a beginning, a middle, and an end.

What You'll Need: Piece of poster board, blunt scissors, marker or pen, letter cards

In this activity, children who have mastered beginning sounds practice listening for letter sounds in other parts of a word.

Cut a piece of poster board approximately 18″ × 6″. Divide it into three sections with a marker or pen. Choose a letter card. Say some words that have that letter at the beginning, middle, and end. For example, for the letter *S,* you might slowly say the words *syrup, messy,* and *bus.* Have the child place the letter card on the beginning, middle, or end section of the letter strip to indicate the *S* sound's position in each word. Select a new letter, and repeat the activity.

FUNNY FARM

Laugh and learn with this silly beginning-sound game.

What You'll Need: Paper, marker or pen

Use children's love of tall tales to practice beginning sounds.

Start a Funny Farm story about an animal on your farm: "I have a gorilla who gulps guppies." Encourage the child to create another sentence. In each sentence, use a lot of words beginning with the initial sound in the animal's name. Take turns making up Funny Farm sentences.

NATURE COLLECTION

▼▼▼

See how many different nature items you can collect and label.

What You'll Need: Small brown bag, collection of nature items (see below), shirt box, self-adhesive notes, marker or pen

Expand a child's environment by helping him or her collect nature objects, display and label those items in a box, and learn beginning sounds.

Go in your backyard or to the park, or take a nature walk with the child, and look for nature objects alphabetically. For example, you could say to the child, "Find something that begins like the word *bird*." (Possible solution: blueberries.) Next you might say, "Find something that begins like *sun*." (Possible solution: seeds.) Continue with other clues to find such items as leaves, a rock, an acorn, or a feather. As you find items, have the child put them in a small brown bag.

When your collecting is complete and you are inside your home, have the child place the collected nature items in a shirt box. Give the child a pad of self-adhesive notes and a marker or pen to write the beginning letter of each item and then place that label by the correct item.

Try this activity at different times of the year and see how the nature items vary.

APPENDIX

PHONOGRAMS

▼▼

A phonogram (FO-no-gram) is a series of letters that is consistently used to form words. The following list contains some of the most commonly used phonograms (and the symbol representing the sound of the key vowel) in the English language. The child should study this list in order to learn some of the many different words derived from the same sounds.

-ace (ā)	-ain (ā)	game	-are (ā)	-eat (ē)	-ight (ī)	-ink (ĭ)	-old (ō)
face	gain	name	bare	beat	fight	link	bold
lace	main	same	care	feat	light	pink	cold
race	pain	tame	dare	heat	might	rink	fold
brace	rain	blame	fare	meat	night	sink	hold
grace	brain	flame	rare	neat	right	wink	sold
place	chain	frame	scare	peat	tight	blink	told
space	drain	shame	share	seat	bright	drink	
	grain		spare	cheat	flight	think	-ot (ŏ)
-ad (ă)	plain	-an (ă)	stare	treat	knight		cot
bad	stain	ban	square	wheat		-ip (ĭ)	got
dad	train	can			-ill (ĭ)	dip	hot
fad	sprain	man	-ave (ā)	-ell (ĕ)	bill	hip	lot
had		pan	cave	bell	fill	lip	not
mad	-ake (ā)	ran	gave	sell	hill	rip	spot
pad	bake	tan	rave	tell	will	tip	
sad	cake	van	save	well	drill	chip	-ow (ou)
glad	fake	bran	wave	yell	grill	drip	bow
	lake	plan	brave	shell	skill	flip	cow
-ail (ā)	make	than	crave	smell	still	ship	how
bail	rake		shave	spell		skip	now
fail	take	-and (ă)			-ing (ĭ)	trip	brow
jail	wake	band	-eak (ē)	-ent (ĕ)	king		plow
mail	brake	hand	beak	bent	ring	-ock (ŏ)	
nail	flake	land	leak	dent	sing	dock	-ow (ō)
pail	shake	sand	peak	rent	wing	lock	bow
rail	snake	bland	weak	sent	bring	rock	low
sail	stake	gland	sneak	tent	swing	sock	row
tail		grand	speak	vent	thing	block	flow
frail	-ame (ā)	stand	squeak	went	spring	clock	show
snail	came	strand	streak	scent	string	flock	slow
trail	fame			spent		knock	snow